Facts About the Tasmanian Devil

By Lisa Strattin

© 2019 Lisa Strattin

FREE BOOK

FREE FOR ALL SUBSCRIBERS

LisaStrattin.com/Subscribe-Here

BOX SET

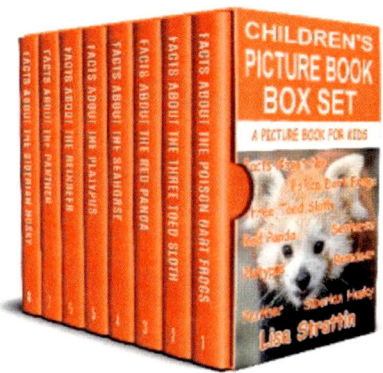

- FACTS ABOUT THE POISON DART FROGS
- FACTS ABOUT THE THREE TOED SLOTH
  - FACTS ABOUT THE RED PANDA
  - FACTS ABOUT THE SEAHORSE
  - FACTS ABOUT THE PLATYPUS
  - FACTS ABOUT THE REINDEER
  - FACTS ABOUT THE PANTHER
- FACTS ABOUT THE SIBERIAN HUSKY

LisaStrattin.com/BookBundle

Facts for Kids Picture Books by Lisa Strattin

Little Blue Penguin, Vol 92

Chipmunk, Vol 5

Frilled Lizard, Vol 39

Blue and Gold Macaw, Vol 13

Poison Dart Frogs, Vol 50

Blue Tarantula, Vol 115

African Elephants, Vol 8

Amur Leopard, Vol 89

Sabre Tooth Tiger, Vol 167

Baboon, Vol 174

Sign Up for New Release Emails Here

LisaStrattin.com/subscribe-here

All rights reserved. No part of this book may be reproduced by any means whatsoever without the written permission from the author, except brief portions quoted for purpose of review.

All information in this book has been carefully researched and checked for factual accuracy. However, the author and publisher makes no warranty, express or implied, that the information contained herein is appropriate for every individual, situation or purpose and assume no responsibility for errors or omissions. The reader assumes the risk and full responsibility for all actions, and the author will not be held responsible for any loss or damage, whether consequential, incidental, special or otherwise, that may result from the information presented in this book.

All images are free for use or purchased from stock photo sites or royalty free for commercial use.

Some coloring pages might be of the general species due to lack of available images.

I have relied on my own observations as well as many different sources for this book and I have done my best to check facts and give credit where it is due. In the event that any material is used without proper permission, please contact me so that the oversight can be corrected.

COVER IMAGE

https://flickr.com/photos/136315829@N03/35649552756/

ADDITIONAL IMAGES

https://www.flickr.com/photos/136315829@N03/35322065450/

https://www.flickr.com/photos/136315829@N03/34847830974/

https://www.flickr.com/photos/floydwilde/3241028074

https://www.flickr.com/photos/nordelch/26924028330/

https://www.flickr.com/photos/nordelch/26592675594/

https://www.flickr.com/photos/dantaylor/334271129/

https://www.flickr.com/photos/136315829@N03/31555552404

https://www.flickr.com/photos/136315829@N03/35583182132/

https://www.flickr.com/photos/shebalso/3525123750

https://www.flickr.com/photos/juliakoefender/6132347367

Contents

INTRODUCTION	9
CHARACTERISTICS	11
APPEARANCE	13
LIFE STAGES	15
LIFE SPAN	17
SIZE	19
HABITAT	21
DIET	23
ENEMIES	25
SUITABILITY AS PETS	27

INTRODUCTION

The Tasmanian Devil is a carnivorous marsupial distantly related to kangaroos and wombats. Although their closest relative is a kangaroo, the Tasmanian devil has the appearance of a wild dog. The Tasmanian Devil is only found on the Australian island state of Tasmania.

CHARACTERISTICS

The Tasmanian Devil is characterized by their black fur and the offensive odor that they secrete when they are stressed. They are also known to make a horrible, loud screeching sound when feeling threatened.

The Tasmanian Devil is known to display odd behavior. When it feels threatened by a predator, or is competing for a mate, they will lunge, while teeth-baring and growling at the enemy. It turns to rage so quickly that this is why European settlers first named it the devil.

APPEARANCE

The Tasmanian Devil is a distinctive black, or very dark brown color, with a white band across its chest. The head is dog-like and the ears are large and pinkish-red.

LIFE STAGES

The females give birth after about three weeks of pregnancy to 20 or 30 very tiny babies. These babies crawl up their mother's fur and into her pouch where they are kept safe as well as fed.

However, only a few of the babies will survive because the mother cannot feed them all at once. The babies leave the safety of their mother's pouch when they are about 4 months old. They are big and strong enough to make it on their own when they are 8 months old.

LIFE SPAN

The Tasmanian Devil lives to be 5 to 8 years old, on average.

SIZE

Male Tasmanian Devils will grow to a total length of around 35 inches including the tail and weigh over 16 pounds. Females rarely exceed 31 inches in length and 13 pounds in weight.

HABITAT

Tasmanian Devils are solitary animals and are nocturnal. They rest in burrows, caves and hollow logs during the day and come out at night to find food. They use their long whiskers and sense of smell to find prey while avoiding predators.

DIET

Tasmanian Devils are carnivorous and prey on snakes, birds, fish, insects and road kill.

When a carcass is found, they are known to be one of the loudest animals when fighting for a meal.

ENEMIES

Tasmanian Devils have only a few natural predators. The main threat to these animals are diseases. The biggest and most obvious hunter of Tasmanian Devils, the Tasmanian Tiger, became extinct many years ago.

Tasmanian Devils used to inhabit much of mainland Australia but are now confined only to the island of Tasmania. Birds of prey, such as owls and eagles, can and do kill them for food. Since owls hunt at night and other raptors during the day, there is no safe time for very small individual animals.

SUITABILITY AS PETS

Tasmanian Devils are not suitable to be pets. They are wild and known to turn from calm to rage in a matter of moments! You might be able to see them in zoos, but they are probably not in every local zoo.

COLOR ME

COLOR ME

COLOR ME

COLOR ME

COLOR ME

COLOR ME

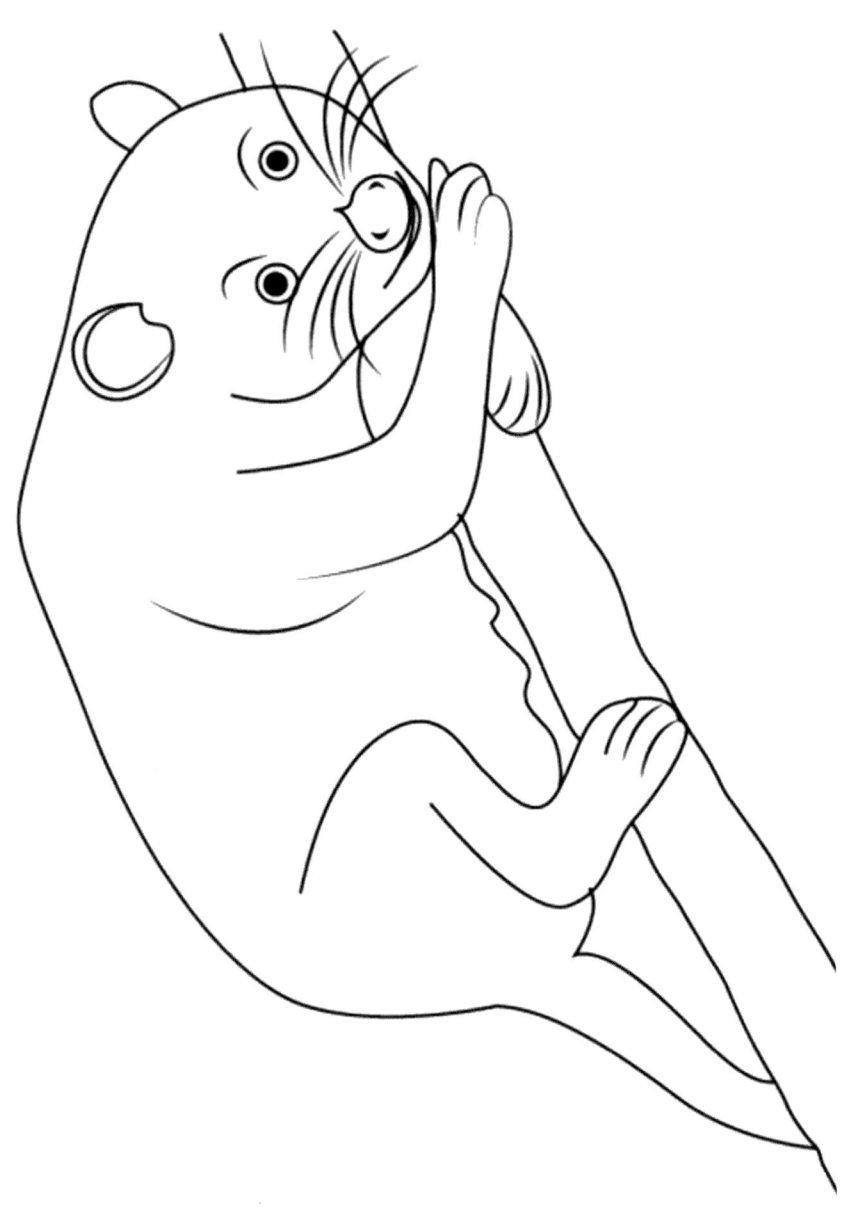

COLOR ME

COLOR ME

COLOR ME

COLOR ME

Please leave me a review here:

LisaStrattin.com/Review-Vol-228

For more Kindle Downloads Visit Lisa Strattin Author Page on Amazon Author Central

amazon.com/author/lisastrattin

To see upcoming titles, visit my website at LisaStrattin.com– most books available on Kindle!

LisaStrattin.com

FREE BOOK

FOR ALL SUBSCRIBERS – SIGN UP NOW

LisaStrattin.com/Subscribe-Here

LisaStrattin.com/Facebook

LisaStrattin.com/Youtube

Made in the USA
Las Vegas, NV
30 October 2021